LOOKING AT COUNTRIES

Looking at
CUBA

Kathleen Pohl

Reading consultant: Susan Nations, M.Ed.,
author/literacy coach/consultant in literacy development

Gareth Stevens
Publishing

Please visit our web site at www.garethstevens.com.
For a free color catalog describing Gareth Stevens Publishing's list
of high-quality books, call 1-800-542-2595 (USA) or 1-800-387-3178 (Canada).
Gareth Stevens Publishing's fax: 1-877-542-2596

Library of Congress Cataloging-in-Publication Data

Pohl, Kathleen.
    Looking at Cuba / Kathleen Pohl.
      p. cm. — (Looking at countries)
    Includes bibliographical references and index.
    ISBN-10: 0-8368-9058-2   ISBN-13: 978-0-8368-9058-7 (lib.bdg)
    ISBN-10: 0-8368-9059-0   ISBN-13: 978-0-8368-9059-4 (softcover)
    1. Cuba—Juvenile literature. I. Title.
F1758.5.P64   2008
972.91—dc22   2008002571

This edition first published in 2009 by
Gareth Stevens Publishing
A Weekly Reader® Company
1 Reader's Digest Road
Pleasantville, NY 10570-7000 USA

Copyright © 2009 by Gareth Stevens, Inc.

Senior Managing Editor: Lisa M. Herrington
Senior Editor: Barbara Bakowski
Creative Director: Lisa Donovan
Designer: Tammy West
Photo Researcher: Charlene Pinckney

Photo credits: (t=top, b=bottom, l=left, r=right, c=center)
Cover Cynthia Carris Alonso; title page Cynthia Carris Alonso; p. 4 Gavin Hellier/Jon Arnold Images/
Alamy; p. 6 Patrick Frilet/Hemis/Corbis; p. 7t Günter Flegar/imagebroker/Alamy; p. 7b Donald Nausbaum/
Corbis; p. 8t Cynthia Carris Alonso; p. 8b Jose Fuste Raga/Corbis; p. 9 Enrique de la Osa/epa/Corbis;
p. 10 Peter Adams Photography/Alamy; p. 11t John Birdsong/CFW Images; p. 11b Rod McLean/Photographers
Direct; p. 12 John Birdsong/CFW Images; p. 13t Peter Turnley for Harper's/Corbis; p. 13b Bob Sacha/Corbis;
p. 14 Jose Fuste Raga/Corbis; p. 15t Cynthia Carris Alonso; p. 15b Lee Lockwood/Time Life Pictures/Getty Images;
p. 16 CFW; p. 17t Steven Vidler/Eurasia Press/Corbis; p. 17b John Sylvester/Alamy; p. 18 David Norton/Alamy;
p. 19t adam eastland /Alamy; p. 19b Ilan Hamra/dpa/Corbis; p. 20t Melvyn Longhurst/Alamy; p. 20b John Birdsall/
CFW Images; p. 21 Shutterstock; p. 22 Peter Adams/Corbis; p. 23t Rainer Hackenberg/zefa/Corbis; p. 23b Cindy Karp/
Getty Images; p. 24 Enrique de la Osa/EFE/epa/Corbis; p. 25t Chris Howes/Wild Places Photography/Alamy;
p. 25b Cynthia Carris Alonso; p. 26 Shutterstock; p. 27t A. Roque/AFP/Getty Images; p. 27b Ferruccio/Alamy

Printed in the United States of America

1 2 3 4 5 6 7 8 9 11 10 09 08

Contents

Words that appear in the glossary are printed in **boldface** type the first time they occur in the text.

Where Is Cuba?

Cuba is an island country south of the United States. Its full name is the Republic of Cuba. It is made up of one big island and thousands of tiny islands. Most Cubans live on the big island. That island is about the size of the state of Pennsylvania.

Did you know?

Cuba is about 90 miles (145 kilometers) south of Key West, Florida.

NORTH AMERICA

UNITED STATES

Atlantic Ocean

CUBA

Pacific Ocean

SOUTH AMERICA

Cuba is the biggest island in the West Indies.

The former National Capitol building in Havana was once the center of government. It is now home to the Academy of Sciences.

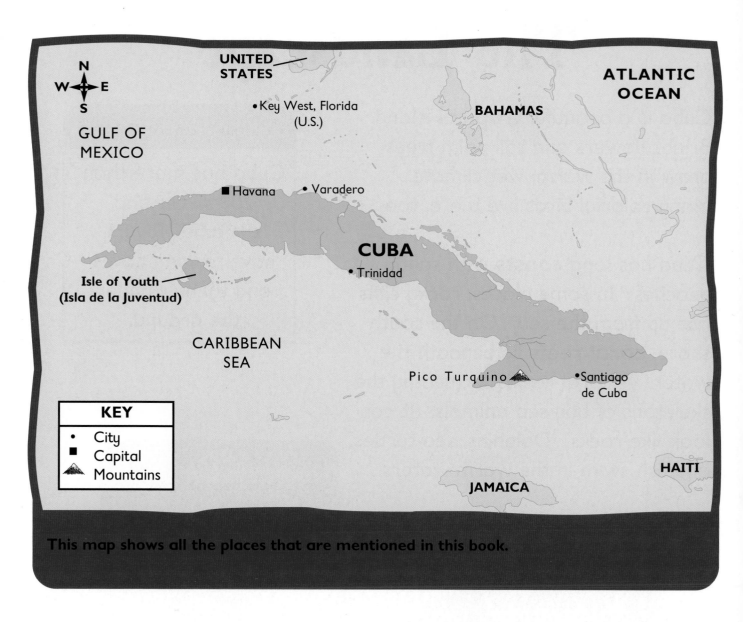

This map shows all the places that are mentioned in this book.

The Caribbean Sea lies to the south of Cuba. The Atlantic Ocean is to the northeast. The Gulf of Mexico is to the northwest. Cuba has other island neighbors. They include the Bahamas to the north. Jamaica is south of Cuba. Haiti lies to the east.

Havana is the capital of Cuba. It is about 500 years old! Havana is the center of government, trade, and the arts.

The Landscape

Cuba is a beautiful **tropical** island. Bright flowers and tall palm trees grow in the warm, wet climate. Many colorful birds live there, too.

Cuba has long **coasts** with sandy beaches. In some places, rocky cliffs rise up from the sea. On the south shore, **coral reefs** lie beneath the water. A coral reef is formed by the skeletons of tiny sea animals. It can look like rocks. Dolphins, sea turtles, and fish swim in the warm waters.

Did you know?

Cuba has more than 200 rivers and streams. Rivers have formed caves and tunnels under the ground.

Cuba is known for its white-sand beaches and sparkling seas.

6

You might have seen flamingos at a zoo. These large pink birds are common in Cuba.

Hills that look like loaves of bread dot the landscape in the west.

Cuba's second-biggest island is the Isle of Youth. It is famous for its black-sand beaches and large pine forests.

Much of Cuba is flat land or gently rolling plains. Mountains rise in three areas of the main island. Pico Turquino, in the southeast, is the tallest peak. In the west, hills with flat tops look like giant loaves of bread!

Weather and Seasons

Cuba's climate is warm and wet, with **trade winds** from the west. Trade winds are winds that blow in the same direction all the time. These winds keep Cuba cooler than most other tropical countries. The average temperature is 77 degrees Fahrenheit (25 degrees Celsius).

Thick rain forests grow in Cuba's warm, wet climate.

Visitors enjoy the soft sands and clear waters of Varadero Beach. Its nickname is Blue Beach. Can you guess why?

Hurricanes often bring strong winds, heavy rains, and high waves to Cuba's coastline.

Cuba has two seasons—a dry season and a rainy season. The sunny, dry season lasts from November to April. During those months, the lack of rain can cause **droughts**. People have little water for drinking and growing crops.

The rainy season runs from May to October. It rains for a short time on most days. Tropical storms can bring strong winds and rain. Storms cause harm to land, crops, and buildings.

Did you know?

Hurricanes usually happen over warm tropical waters, like those that surround Cuba. The country gets a hurricane every one to two years. Winds can cause high waves that flood the coast.

Cuban People

More than 11 million people live in Cuba. Native peoples lived there first. Then Spain ruled Cuba for about 400 years. The Spanish brought slaves from Africa. Today, most Cubans come from a mix of these backgrounds. Spanish is the main language of Cuba.

Cuba is a **communist** country. There are no free elections. The government controls how much money people can make. It owns most of the land and the businesses.

Did you know?

Each year, many people flee, or leave, from Cuba by boat. They try to reach the United States, often to look for a better way of life.

People in Cuba mostly wear casual Western-style clothing. Women sometimes wear brightly colored traditional outfits for holidays and festivals.

Girls in costume have fun marching in a parade.

The ancestors of most Cubans came to the island from Spain and Africa.

The government provides people with free schooling and health care. They also get low-cost food and housing.

During the past 50 years, Cubans were not always free to worship as they chose. Today, however, people can go to church. Four out of 10 Cubans are Roman Catholic. Some others are Protestant, and a few are Jewish. Others practice a religion called Santeria. It is a mix of Catholic and traditional African beliefs.

School and Family

Education is important in Cuba. Children must go to school from the ages of six to 16. Public school is free for everyone. There are no private schools.

Children go to primary school until age 12. They study math, history, and reading. They learn some English, too. Then students go on to secondary school. Most Cuban teenagers live

At school, students get a lesson in using computers.

Many children walk to school, like these two girls in Havana.

This family enjoys music and dancing—right at home!

at **boarding schools** in the countryside. The students must spend a certain amount of time working in farm fields.

Most families are small, with one or two children. Cuba's laws say that women and men have the same rights and duties for housework and child care. Many women work outside the home. About half of the country's doctors and scientists are women.

Country Life

Most Cubans who live in the country work on small farms. Crops grow well in the country's rich soil. Farmers grow fruits and vegetables and raise beef cattle.

The government owns most of the large farms. The main **cash crops** are sugarcane, tobacco, and coffee. (Cash crops are grown to be sold, not used by the farmers.) Tobacco is used to make cigars. Cuba **exports** cigars, selling and shipping them to other countries.

A farmhouse sits among palm trees in this mountain valley in the west.

This worker cuts sugarcane. Sugarcane is the most important food crop in Cuba.

Fishing boats dock in Havana's harbor with the day's catch.

On the coast, some people fish for a living. Fleets of fishing boats go out to sea. They catch tuna, lobsters, and shrimp.

City Life

Eight out of every 10 Cubans live in cities. More than 2 million people live in Havana, the capital. It is the largest city in Cuba. Some of the city's forts and castles are 500 years old! Many of the buildings in the old part of the city need repairs.

Few cars and buses travel the streets of Havana. Most people cannot afford to own cars.

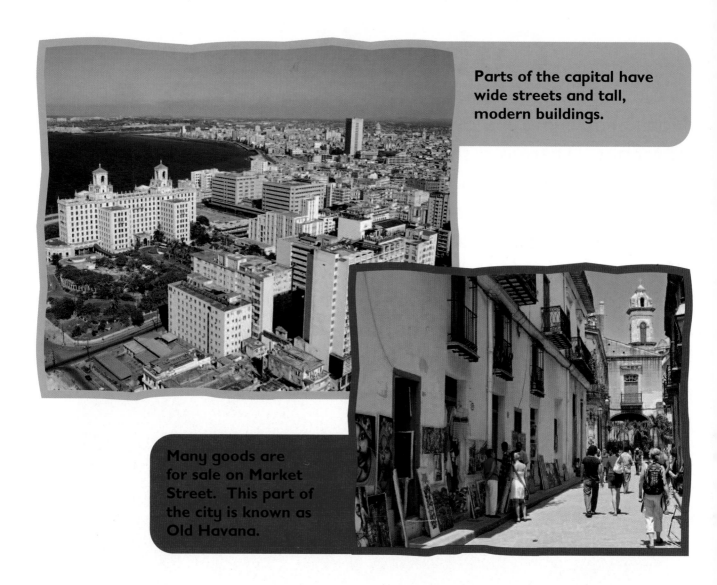

Parts of the capital have wide streets and tall, modern buildings.

Many goods are for sale on Market Street. This part of the city is known as Old Havana.

Havana has modern hotels, offices, and museums, too. It is the home of the world-famous Cuban National Ballet. The city has many parks and plazas, or town squares.

Havana is also a busy **seaport**. Goods are shipped into and out of Cuba through Havana.

The second-biggest city is Santiago de Cuba, in the southeast. The city sits on high hills above a large bay. It is a busy port with many historic buildings.

Cuban Houses

Many people in Cuba own their homes. Some houses are in need of repairs. There is a shortage of new houses, too. It costs a lot to bring building materials to Cuba by boat from countries far away. The United States is a close neighbor. Because of past disagreements, the United States does not allow trade with Cuba.

In the countryside, many people live in small wood huts with dirt floors. The huts are called **bohíos**. They have **thatched** roofs

Houses in the town of Trinidad have a Spanish look. They are painted in bright colors and have red tile roofs.

made from palm leaves. Other houses are made of brick or cement. Some homes have no plumbing or power for lights.

In the cities, some people rent apartments owned by the government. Many of the buildings are crowded and run-down. The renters do not pay much money. Sometimes two families share one small apartment.

In the cities, some people live in apartments. They like to sit on their balconies, or upper porches.

In the countryside, most people live in small huts with thatched roofs.

Did you know?

Most bohíos have only two rooms. A separate hut is used for cooking.

Cuban Food

Food is not plentiful in Cuba. The government **rations** food, supplying it in small amounts so that there is some for everyone. People stand in line to buy rice, beans, meat, and eggs at grocery stores called **bodegas**. Some Cubans shop at outdoor markets, too. Food costs more there.

PRECIO

PRECIO
70

PRECIO
70

Dried beans and lentils are for sale at a street market.

People sometimes shop at outdoor markets for fresh vegetables.

Black beans and rice are common foods at the dinner table.

Most Cubans eat a lot of rice and beans. They also eat boniato, a kind of sweet potato. Spicy stews made with garlic, peppers, and onions are common. Picadillo (pee-kah-DEE-yoh) is a dish made with ground beef, tomatoes, and olives. People eat fruits such as mangoes and plantains, which are like bananas. Coffee is a popular drink at every meal.

Did you know?

Black beans are sometimes called turtle beans. They are used in many Cuban dishes, especially soups.

At Work

Farming was once the biggest business in Cuba. Today, however, many more people work in **tourism**. Visitors from all over the world come to Cuba to enjoy its beaches. They come to swim and sail, to fish and scuba dive. Many Cubans work in hotels and restaurants. They drive taxis or work as tour guides.

Did you know?

About 300,000 people in Cuba have jobs in tourism. About 2 million people from other countries visit Cuba each year.

However, the United States does not allow Americans to travel to Cuba because of poor relations with its government.

Tourism is a big business in Cuba. Many workers cook or serve food in restaurants, such as the café shown here.

A farmworker harvests a field of sugarcane. Most farm machinery in Cuba is old. Workers often cut sugarcane by hand.

Some people work in health clinics or hospitals. All Cubans get free health care.

Some Cubans work in stores, banks, or offices. Some are doctors or nurses. Others teach school or work in factories. People work in mining and logging, too. The country's **natural resources** include copper and wood. Cuba exports sugarcane, a metal called nickel, and cigars.

Having Fun

Salsa is a fast dance with a strong beat that is popular in Cuba. Cubans like jazz music, too. Many great jazz musicians have come from Cuba.

Baseball was introduced in Cuba about 150 years ago. It was brought by American sailors and by Cubans who had been to the

Did you know?

Cuban boxers have won many Olympic gold medals.

Batter up! Like American children, Cuban kids love to play baseball!

People rent sailboats at Cuba's beautiful beaches.

These Cuban musicians play traditional drums.

United States. Baseball is the number-one sport in Cuba. Cubans are very proud of their national team. They like basketball, volleyball, and soccer, too. Cubans of all ages play sports in parks and in the streets.

In summer, Cubans celebrate a festival called Carnival. It marks the end of the sugar harvest. People enjoy music, fireworks, and parades of floats and costumed dancers. Lively parties take place in Santiago de Cuba and Havana.

Cuba: The Facts

• The official name of Cuba is República de Cuba, or Republic of Cuba.

• Cuba is a communist country. Its government owns most of the businesses. The government also controls the schools, health services, and transportation.

• Cuba celebrates Liberation Day on January 1. The holiday marks the day in 1959 when rebels led by Fidel Castro defeated the country's government. Fidel Castro led Cuba from 1959 to February 2008.

• In 2008, Fidel Castro's brother Raúl was elected president. The president is the **chief of state** and the head of the government.

The flag of Cuba has three blue bars and two white bars. A white star sits on a red triangle on the left side of the flag.

• The National Assembly of People's Power makes the country's laws and elects its leaders.

• In 1962, the United States stopped trading, or exchanging goods, with Cuba. The U.S. government did that because it disapproved of Cuba's actions.

• The explorer Christopher Columbus landed in Cuba in 1492. Spain ruled Cuba for more than 400 years.

Did you know?

The smallest hummingbird in the world lives in Cuba! The bee hummingbird measures only about 2 inches (5 centimeters) long.

Fidel Castro (left) led Cuba from 1959 to 2008. In February 2008, his brother Raúl Castro became president.

Cuba's unit of money is the **peso.**

Glossary

ancestors — family members who lived in the past

boarding schools — schools where children live away from home

bodegas — government-owned stores where people in Cuba buy food at low prices

bohíos — small wood huts with thatched roofs

cash crops — crops that are grown and sold to make money

chief of state — the main representative of a country

coasts — the areas of land along bodies of water such as oceans or seas

communist — a system of government in which one party rules. The government owns most of the businesses and controls goods and services.

coral reefs — the skeletons of tiny animals called coral polyps (PAH-lips) that live in warm sea waters, often near the shore

droughts — long periods without rain, which can cause water shortages and damage to crops

exports — sells and ships goods to other countries

natural resources — things supplied by nature, such as oil or wood, that are used by people

peso — the unit of money in Cuba

rations — limits amounts of food or other items, often because supplies are short

salsa — a fast, rhythmic dance that is popular in Latin American countries

seaport — a town or city on the ocean or sea where goods are shipped in and out

thatched — made of woven bundles of grass, palm leaves, or straw

tourism — a business that serves people who travel for fun

trade winds — winds that blow steadily from one direction at sea

tropical — having a hot and wet climate

Find Out More

Enchanted Learning: Central America and the Caribbean
www.littleexplorers.com/geography/centamer

EnchantedLearning: Coral Reef Animal Printouts
www.enchantedlearning.com/biomes/coralreef/coralreef.shtml

Fact Monster: Cuba

www.factmonster.com/country/profiles/cuba.html

National Geographic Magazine: Cuba Naturally

ngm.nationalgeographic.com/ngm/0311/feature4/index.html

Publisher's note to educators and parents: Our editors have carefully reviewed these Web sites to ensure that they are suitable for children. Many Web sites change frequently, however, and we cannot guarantee that a site's future contents will continue to meet our high standards of quality and educational value. Be advised that children should be closely supervised whenever they access the Internet.

My Map of Cuba

Photocopy or trace the map on page 31. Then write in the names of the countries, bodies of water, cities, and land areas listed below. (Look at the map on page 5 if you need help.)

After you have written in the names of all the places, find some crayons and color the map!

Countries
Cuba
Jamaica
Haiti
Bahamas
United States

Bodies of Water
Atlantic Ocean
Caribbean Sea
Gulf of Mexico

Cities
Havana
Santiago de Cuba
Key West, Florida (U.S.)
Trinidad
Varadero

Islands and Mountains
Isle of Youth (Isla de la Juventud)
Pico Turquino

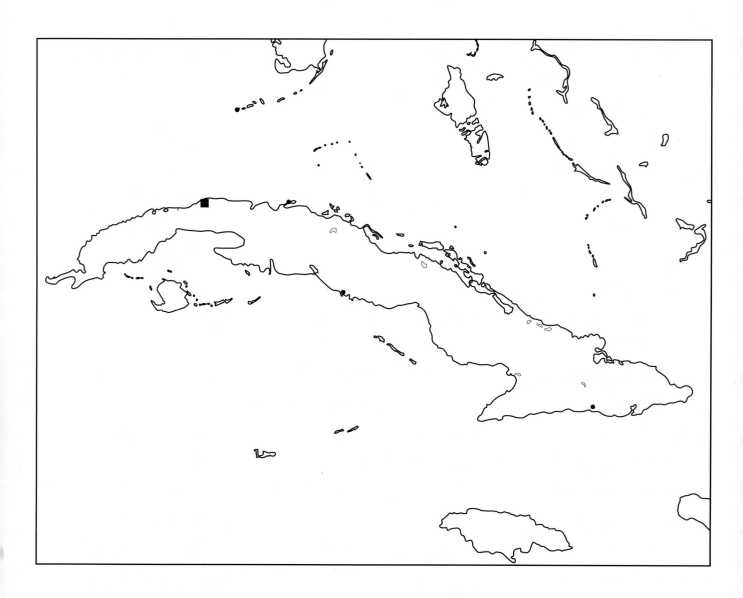

Index